Upper Yosemite Fall, Spring. The combination of Upper Fall (1,430 feet), Lower Fall (320 feet), and the intermediate cascades (675 feet) plunging over Yosemite Valley's north rim form North America's highest waterfall. Yosemite Creek drains a relatively small area of predominately nonabsorbent granite, consequently during most years Yosemite Falls thunders mightily under heavy spring/early-summer melt but usually dwindle to a trickle by late-summer.

From THE YOSEMITE ULTIMATE PARK PRINT® BOOK

SIERRA PRESS, INC.

PHOTO © WILLIAM NEILL

El Capitan, Mid-Winter Morning. El Capitan is the world's tallest exposed granite monolith, twice the height of the Rock of Gibraltar. The sheer face of El Capitan rises 3,000 feet above Yosemite Valley with the summit being an additional 600 feet above its vertical rise. It is composed of extremely hard granite and, consequently, was better able to resist the grinding and gouging force of glaciers.

From THE YOSEMITE ULTIMATE PARK PRINT® BOOK

SIERRA PRESS, INC.

PHOTO © ANNETTE BOTTARO-WALKLET/QUIETWORKS

El Capitan and Half Dome, Sunset Light. Boldly shaped rock forms such as El Capitan and Half Dome are both fascinating and perplexing. The granite that forms Yosemite's peaks and domes was formed from molten rock at the roots of ancient volcanoes. Following uplifts, which were the result of tectonic and seismic activity, the overlying sedimentary layers were stripped away by erosion, leaving the harder granites exposed. The sculpting power of glaciers and erosion led to the formations seen today.

From THE YOSEMITE ULTIMATE PARK PRINT® BOOK

SIERRA PRESS, INC.

PHOTO © LARRY ULRICH

Giant Sequoias, Mariposa Grove. When judged by total mass and volume, the giant sequoia *(Sequoiadendron giganteum)* is the world's largest living thing. Single limbs of mature trees are often larger than the trunks of record-size trees of many other species. Its trunk is stout and column-like and has thick, cinnamon colored bark that is extremely fire resistant. There appear to be no built-in limits to growth for these trees since they do not die of old age.

From THE YOSEMITE ULTIMATE PARK PRINT® BOOK

SIERRA PRESS, INC.

PHOTO © LARRY ULRICH

Wildflowers in Tuolumne Meadows. At an elevation of 8,600 feet, Tuolumne Meadows is the largest subalpine meadow in the Sierra Nevada. These lush meadows were the result of a "little ice age" about 2,500 years ago, which raised the water table and killed the forest that existed at the time. Wildflowers usually bloom from early-July through mid-August marking a spring-like season normally experienced during April and May at lower elevations.

From THE YOSEMITE ULTIMATE PARK PRINT® BOOK

SIERRA PRESS, INC.

PHOTO © LARRY ULRICH

Valley View and Winter Sunset. Located at a turnout at the western end of Yosemite Valley, this is one of the most impressive vistas in the world. It provides the classic view of western Yosemite Valley including El Capitan, Merced River, Three Graces, Bridalveil Fall, and, far in the background, Half Dome. This viewpoint was previously known as Gates of the Valley since it was the first view of Yosemite Valley experienced by early visitors entering via the Old Big Oak Flat Road.

From THE YOSEMITE ULTIMATE PARK PRINT® BOOK

SIERRA PRESS, INC.

PHOTO © GALEN ROWELL/MOUNTAIN LIGHT

Jeffrey Pine on Sentinel Dome at Sunset. Following a short, 1.1 mile, hike to the summit of Sentinel Dome one is treated to seeing the skeletal remains of a *"krummholtzed"* Jeffrey Pine. This valiant tree waged a prolonged battle against the elements at the upper limits of its normal habitat until the late-1970's when it lost its final struggle. Today, with its bark stripped away, it stands as a monument to the fragility of life above 7,000 feet.

From THE YOSEMITE ULTIMATE PARK PRINT® BOOK

SIERRA PRESS, INC.

PHOTO © HOWARD WEAMER

Bridalveil Fall and Merced River, Autumn. This waterfall drops 620 feet into an alcove at the western end of Yosemite Valley. The fall was created when the bed of the Merced River, into which it flows, was lowered by erosion and glaciation. This left Bridalveil Creek suspended above, creating a classic example of a "hanging valley." It received today's name when early explorers observed swirling winds blowing its base into a broad, delicate mist resembling that of a bridal train.

From THE YOSEMITE ULTIMATE PARK PRINT® BOOK

SIERRA PRESS, INC.

PHOTO © LARRY ULRICH

Vernal Fall, Spring. The Merced River plunges 317 feet prior to reaching the tranquillity of Yosemite Valley. It passes over a broad precipice spreading a sheet of water up to 80 feet wide. Prior to this fall, the water of the Merced River leapt over 594-foot Nevada Fall. When viewed from Glacier Point, Vernal and Nevada falls appear as steps on what is known as the Giant's Stairway.

From THE YOSEMITE ULTIMATE PARK PRINT® BOOK

SIERRA PRESS, INC.

PHOTO © HOWARD WEAMER

FIRST
CLASS
POSTAGE
REQUIRED

Yosemite Falls and Merced River, Winter. "The River of Our Lady of Mercy," as it was named by early Spaniard explorers, meanders through the relatively flat and narrow Yosemite Valley. With its headwaters near Mt. Lyell and the Park's southern boundary, the Merced River drains a large watershed area. It was granted Wild and Scenic status by Congress and is the only major Sierran river that remains undammed prior to reaching the San Joaquin Valley.

From THE YOSEMITE ULTIMATE PARK PRINT® BOOK

SIERRA PRESS, INC.

PHOTO © PAT O'HARA

Mule Deer and Cow Parsnip. The most commonly seen large mammal in Yosemite is the California mule deer (*Odocoileus hemionus*). They are migratory according to the season, but can be readily found browsing upon grasses, leaves, wildflowers, and the tender buds of certain shrubs and trees along the margins and in the meadows of Yosemite Valley.

From THE YOSEMITE ULTIMATE PARK PRINT® BOOK

SIERRA PRESS, INC.

PHOTO © MICHAEL FRYE

Half Dome from Stoneman Meadow, Autumn. When viewed from Glacier Point, one realizes that Half Dome is, indeed, more than half of a dome. It is actually a thin, elongated ridge of granite with steep, nearly equal sides. The missing northwest face was probably undercut by a small glacier, leaving the upper portion to be quarried by tens of thousands of freeze-thaw cycles. Ultimately gravity overcame granite and the baseless portion sloughed away.

SIERRA PRESS, INC.

From THE YOSEMITE ULTIMATE PARK PRINT® BOOK

PHOTO © LARRY ULRICH